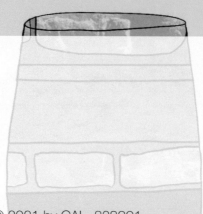

To order additional copies of this book, contact:
Xlibris
844-714-8691
www.Xlibris.com
Orders@Xlibris.com

ISBN: Softcover   978-1-6641-6997-5
        EBook   978-1-6641-6996-8

Library of Congress Control Number: 2021908167

Print information available on the last page.

Rev. date: 04/15/2021

THOUGHTS IN THE EARLY MORN

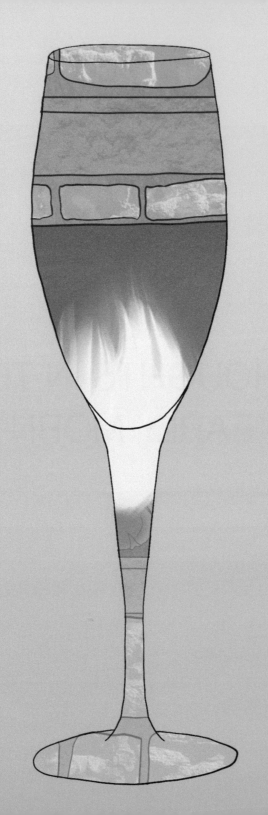

I want a friend and a confidant
I want a partner and an adviser

I want someone who will walk
Through life beside me, sometimes ahead
Never behind me!

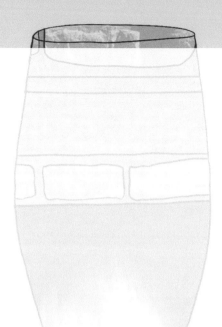

I want someone who can possess my soul
Someone who will haunt my dreams
And will firmly but warmly
Hold my heart in his hand

I want a lover, both spiritually and physically

I want a man who knows the difference
Between having sex and making love

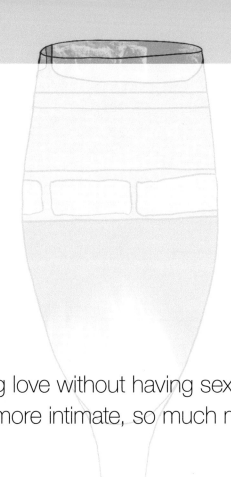

Making love without having sex can be
So much more intimate, so much more fulfilling

I want someone with an opinion
But doesn't force it on anyone

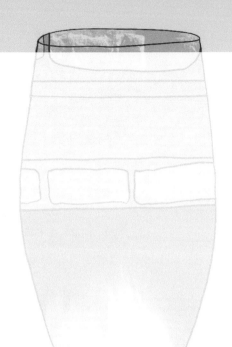

I want a man who can take a little hell when he deserves it
One who can put me in my place when I need it
But never in the presence of others

I want someone who will smile as he sleeps
When I roll over in the night to kiss his shoulder
And tell him that I love him
To cuddle up to him as I go back to sleep

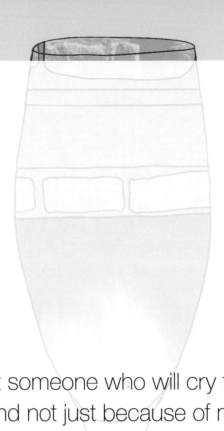

I want someone who will cry for me
And not just because of me

I want a strong, independent man
Who doesn't need me but instead wants me

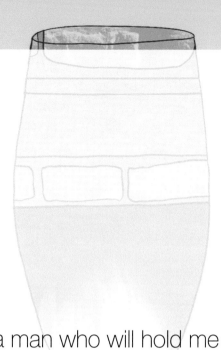

I want a man who will hold me so tight
When I really need some support
When no words are needed
To just let me cry

And the warmth and strength of his arms
Will dry up all the tears
And he will be there for me as I need him

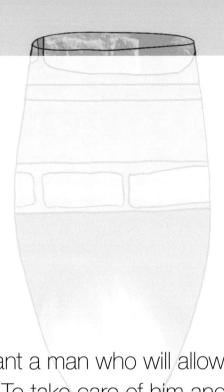

I want a man who will allow me
To take care of him and
Let me hold him just because I want to

And a man who will take care
Of me with all the love he has

I want someone who will have a
Glass of wine with me

As we walk
Hand in hand together on the beach
And watch the incredible sunset

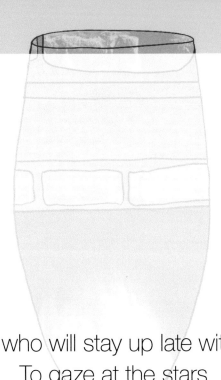

One who will stay up late with me
To gaze at the stars
After midnight
They're brighter then!

I want a man who will appreciate
The smaller things in life

Like the gift of his favorite meal
And his choice of movie with wine
And a roaring fire to warm us

To walk down the street
And laugh as we run in the rain
Getting soaking wet and still
Holding each other's hands

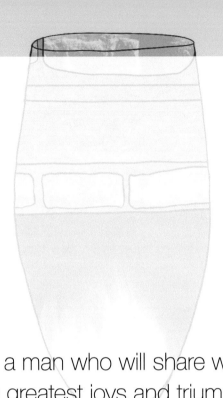

I want a man who will share with me
His greatest joys and triumphs
His deepest sorrows and disappointments

One who will listen to mine
And not judge me because of them

I want a man who will love me
As much as I love him

I will love him
With every fiber of my being!

I want someone who will hold me when I die . . .

Printed in the United States
by Baker & Taylor Publisher Services